THE COMPELLING PROPOSAL

The Compelling Proposal

MAKE IT EASY FOR THE CUSTOMER TO

Buy from You

Steve Thompson

VALUE LIFECYCLE™

THE COMPELLING PROPOSAL
Make it Easy for the Customer to Buy From You!

ISBN   978-1-5445-0410-0 *Paperback*
        978-1-5445-0411-7 *Ebook*

Contents

Contents

Foreword

This book is for sales management and sales professionals who make their living in the B2B world, those whose business is finding, positioning, proposing, negotiating, and closing deals with other businesses. While most of the key concepts presented here apply to selling in general, in these pages we will focus on B2B sales. In the last twenty years, I have developed and grown my consulting business around B2B deals (for selling *and* buying organizations), covering more than $15 billion in business deals in over 120 different industries on every continent except Antarctica—but I'm game if anyone has an opportunity there!

One of the challenges sellers face is that not all deals are created equal. Typically, a small number of deals and accounts make up the vast majority of revenue or new bookings and are often called "must-win." In short, these are the deals that make or break a quarter or year. Yet selling into these situations is only getting more complex. Customers have more access to information on not just what you sell but to other customers who have bought from you. Adding to the burden, the solutions being offered are getting more complex. The number of key buying influencers on the customer side is growing, making the sale more complex while introducing a huge dose of uncertainty into the equation. Who are all these influencers, what's important to each of them, and what if they are not fully aligned? (I can almost guarantee they aren't.)

While sellers bemoan how difficult it is to sell into this complexity, uncertainty, and risk, rarely do they consider that *these issues are typically magnified on the buyer's side*. After all, the buyer is preparing to commit a large sum of money and take on a lot of political risk if the buying decision is not the right one. I have observed that salespeople who can manage the uncertainty, reduce the risk, and make it easier for the customer to make a decision *they feel comfortable with* are more likely to win the business—and win it quickly.

As we discussed in the previous book, *The Irresistible Value Proposition*, our value proposition will go a long way toward cutting through the complexity, uncertainty, and doubt and at least get the customer excited about what we are selling—perhaps even excited enough to want what we are selling now! However, there is a large gap between *wanting* and making the actual decision to *buy*, and these are topics for other books (see the sidebar).

This book is number three in the five-part *Must-Win Deals* series. The first book addressed must-win deals and described the four key things we, as sellers, do to make it challenging for customers to award us critical deals. We also explored the idea of pursuing not just any deal, but a great deal. The second book, *The Irresistible Value Proposition*, dealt with the often-misunderstood concept of value and the development of a value proposition that will excite the customer about what you're selling and make them want it now. This book is concerned with using the proposal to bridge your selling activities and the negotiation, and in the process reinforce trust and credibility, make it easy for the customer to choose you (and feel it is the right choice for them), and manage the uncertainty inherent in the real world. The fourth book in the series, *The Painless Negotiation*, explores negotiating and capturing the value in not just any deal, but a great deal for you and your customer. The final title, *Can't-Lose Accounts*, delves into delivering the promised value, which makes renewals simple, referrals enthusiastic, and upselling and cross-selling much easier. I hope you derive great value from this journey!

As I mentioned previously, about half of my work is with buying organizations, where I help position and close critical deals with key suppliers. A normal part of this job is to review supplier proposals—a task I'm none too fond of. Why? Because I can already tell you what virtually every supplier proposal will say. It will be all about the supplier and their products, services, features (sometimes benefits), office locations, growth, recent acquisitions, etc. I don't know how the math works, but somehow each supplier is number one in their field. They're all innovative, world-leading, Gartner upper-right quadrant, etc. It's no wonder customers have a hard time choosing one supplier over another and often just go with one of two "safe" choices: the lowest price or simply not awarding the business to anyone!

The problem is that these proposals are constructed more as marketing documents than ones meant to close a sale. Therefore, the theory (the marketing rule of more views) is that the more pages the better. More pictures, more diagrams, more tables, etc. They are self-defeating because they end up making it harder for the customer to make an informed decision: *nothing in the mountain of data is directly and clearly linked to the outcomes the customer wants to achieve.* As a result, customers begin to question why certain elements are in the proposal, which requires the sales rep to spend more energy justifying the contents of the proposal rather than closing the deal.

The solution is an *outcome-based, compelling proposal* that makes it much easier for the customer to make an informed decision—and feel that it is the right decision for them. My clients have used this simple, powerful format to close deals from as little as $20 thousand to well over $1 billion. It is important to note that most of these proposals are presented early in the sales cycle, which helps the customer focus in on what is really important to them.

Once the customer decides on the direction they want to take, *then* my clients present them with a formal written proposal with all the pictures, charts, graphs, diagrams, terms, SOW, etc. But all that these more detailed proposals do is *document what has already been decided*! The business has already been awarded by key decision makers who were compelled to move ahead by the initial, straightforward, seven-page, compelling proposal. And that is the subject of this book.

* * *

Over more than two decades I have enjoyed the challenge of working with tens of thousands of professionals in sales, sales management, and executive management, ranging from Fortune 100 to small, privately held companies. Not only has this given me access to some of the most successful sales organizations in business today, but I consider it a privilege to call many of these individuals my friends. If you are one of them, then I owe you a debt of gratitude, for it is likely that I learned more from you than I was ever able to give back. I hope this book will begin to repay that debt to future generations of sales professionals.

CHAPTER 1

The Current State of B2B Proposals

*Making It Difficult for
Customers to Choose You*

I remember it like it was yesterday, though it was a dozen or more years ago. One of my key clients was fretting over an upcoming renewal with one of their largest customers. But it was more than a renewal because the customer was taking the business out to bid for the first time in five years, and the bidding was between my client and their largest (and most formidable) competitor.

The format was pretty straightforward. An evaluation team from the customer (headed by an SVP selected by the CEO) would visit my client's headquarters in about a week for a three-hour proposal presentation. The following day the same evaluation team would fly out to meet with the competitor.

I was contacted by the SVP of sales (my primary contact) and asked to preview the presentation the account team had prepared in collaboration with operations and the marketing department. It was slick: approximately sixty slides with terrific graphics and animation detailing the history and superb capabilities of my client. But slick or not, sixty slides in three hours is a lot to stay awake for. What's more, as the presentation droned on, I noticed that the customer wasn't mentioned until *slide forty-eight*. In fact, of the sixty slides in the deck, only nine mentioned or pertained to the customer.

Afterward, I was asked to give my assessment of the presentation. Steeling myself for a tough conversation, I first congratulated them on an outstanding *technical* presentation. Their delivery was smooth, practiced, and showed a mastery of the material. But I did have a few questions:

→ How long had this customer been doing business with my client?
  Answer: fifteen years.
→ The customer was going to the trouble and expense of flying a team of six people, including a senior executive, to our corporate headquarters. Did we know their goals and objectives for the meeting?

Answer: Upon further reflection, we weren't sure.

→ Did we know what was important to the SVP, how big a priority it was, and how he would measure success if he entered into a new contract with us?

Answer: After much hemming and hawing, we realized that we really didn't know.

Based on their answers, I recommended that we quickly change course, reasoning the following.

1. The customer already knew who we were and what we did.
2. We needed to reach out to the evaluation team immediately to determine their objectives for the meeting to avoid wasting their time.
3. We needed to do the same thing with the SVP, who was the key buying influencer.
4. We couldn't afford to waste a golden opportunity with all the customer's key decision makers in the room. We had a captive audience and it would be a shame if we didn't use this opportunity to learn more about what was *important to them.* What's more, it would be risky to assume that everyone on the customer's evaluation team was in agreement on what they wanted to achieve, much less what a great deal looked like.

I consoled the account team with the good news: we only needed a handful of slides, and looking at the current presentation, we had plenty of material to use for the couple of slides that would be about us. Then I had to share the bad news. We were missing critical material for the remaining slides that concerned the customer—and we had a lot of work to do in a short period of time to pull that together. Not surprisingly, my recommendations came as quite a shock to this experienced account team, but at the urging of the SVP of sales, they revamped their entire approach.

The following week, the presentation (which in truth was designed as a dialogue) went off without a hitch and was deemed extremely successful. In fact, at the end of the meeting, the SVP of operations for the customer approached the SVP of sales for my client and said that of the hundreds of supplier presentations he had seen over the years, this one had by far been the best. My client did not give the customer everything they asked for—they were not expecting that—but by shortening the presentation and focusing more on demonstrating an understanding of the customer's needs and challenges, they were able to make a very positive impression. After the presentation, the SVP of operations said that he saw no reason why my client would not be selected again. Now, that was a positive sign!

Fast-forward six months. The customer renewal had been won, and the entire sales organization was in Las Vegas for the annual sales kickoff. I was there and shared the stage during one keynote session with executives from three of my client's largest customers. One of these executives was the SVP of operations on the evaluation team for the renewal we had just won, and I seized the opportunity to ask him some questions during the rehearsal. He reiterated that it was the best proposal presentation he had ever seen. The format had helped him and the evaluation team focus and agree on what was truly important to them in the deal. He was also surprised that my client had shared what was important to *them* in the deal. He had never seen this before, but it really helped the evaluation team see how a deal could be done that was *good for both sides*. He added that being given options by a seller was a rare occurrence for him and the team; it made them feel they were being given the opportunity to choose what worked best for them. It is worth noting that the positive experience this executive and his team had is a common outcome of using the compelling proposal template.

I then asked him what happened when the evaluation team traveled the following day to see the competitor's presentation. Rolling his eyes, he said there must have been over sixty slides (his exact words), and they were almost all about the competitor and their business! What's more, his team was given only one option. When I asked him what he felt during the presentation, he said that about thirty minutes in, he knew my client had won the business, and for the remainder of the presentation he did his best not to nod off.

This is just one of many examples I could share with you, drawn from thousands of deals I have worked on over the years with my clients. In every instance, the proposal presentation was one of the critical conversations that resulted in the win. Did we win every deal? No, but our win rate topped 80 percent, an outstanding number for just about any sales organization. What's more, we were able to grow the size of many deals—sometimes doubling or even tripling them!

My goal in this book is to share what a compelling proposal looks like from the perspective that matters most—your customer's. This will help you increase your win rates and grow the size of your deals. But before we can go there, we need to briefly put the compelling proposal presentation in the proper context. When selling, you cannot afford to view the proposal as an isolated event to be completed just to "check the box" near the end of the sales cycle. Rather, you should view it in the context of the desired ongoing business relationship and as an opportunity to manage the complexity and uncertainty inherent in a B2B deal.

CHAPTER 2

Managing Uncertainty

So It Doesn't Manage You

Let's start the discussion of uncertainty and risk by first determining where the compelling proposal comes into the customer's journey through the Value Lifecycle™. As Figure 2.1 illustrates, it serves as the crucial bridge between creating value (selling) and capturing value (negotiating) in a great deal. As you will learn in the next book in this series, it also serves the purpose of setting up the "right negotiation," putting you in the best position to negotiate the right way.

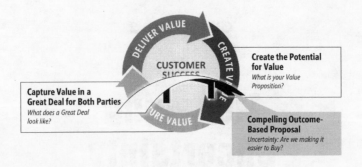

Figure 2.1: The Compelling Outcome-Based Proposal

As you move from creating value to capturing value, you won't always have perfect information. That's because, as you may have noticed, the real world does not always follow a clean and logical path. Because you are dealing with actual people, the real world is fraught with uncertainty and conflicting priorities that lead to risk—for both you and the customer. For example:

→ Who are all the customer's buying influencers?
→ What are the outcomes important to the customer and each key buying influencer?
→ What alternative are you really competing against?
→ What is important to you in a deal?
→ What is the actual "budget" and approval process?
→ What do you do when the customer presents conflicting priorities such as "lowest unit cost" but also "no

volume commitment"? Or they want the "total solution" but have a "limited budget"?

Maybe you're not clear about the alternative you're competing against. If it's a competitor, perhaps you don't know how they will behave or the strategy they will adopt. Are you sure you've met with all the key buying influencers on the customer's side, and do you really know all the outcomes important to them? Are all these influencers aligned on the same outcomes important to the business? Are you *internally* aligned on what is important to your business in a deal?

As you can see, the uncertainties can quickly pile up! Almost *certain*, on the other hand, are the negative implications if you lose the deal (your alternative)! Is this starting to sound like the real world of B2B sales?

If so, wait—there's more!

Let's add in the uncertainty of whether the budget is firm and secure and whether all the customer's buying steps are fully known. Now add the conflicting priorities the customer says are important. They want the lowest unit cost but are not prepared to commit to any minimum volumes. (That will be tough to sell internally.) Or the customer is thrilled with the outcomes you can provide with your total solution, but they only have so much budget. (There's no way you can accomplish both and stay in business for long.)

Now you're really starting to look—and feel—like the real world.

So here's the question you must answer: With all this uncertainty and risk, why would you present *just one option* to your customer in a proposal? Given the dire consequences of losing the deal, do you really think one option will carry the day? The degree to which you are not one hundred percent certain your one option will prevail is the degree to which you are *hoping* it will, and we all know that "hope is not a strategy."

Thankfully, there's a better way!

MULTIPLE ACCEPTABLE OPTIONS

Giving the customer options is a central component of the compelling proposal—and a key tool for managing uncertainty and risk. However, this is not one of those times when you can just "throw it against the wall to see if it sticks." How you construct and present your multiple acceptable options is very important, as Figure 2.2 illustrates.

MULTIPLE ACCEPTABLE OPTIONS
Two or Three Bundled Offers to Manage Uncertainty

- We are prepared to accept any one of them, however...
- We expect the Customer will value each very differently
- Titled to be meaningful to the Customer (Outcomes / Value Proposition)
- Tells us what is really important to the Customer
- Allows the Customer to "Buy" versus us "Selling"
- Encourages the Customer to take ownership of "their Deal"
- Minimize single issue such as "price only" negotiations

Present as *early as possible* in the Sales Cycle

Figure 2.2: Multiple Acceptable Options

Each option should be equally acceptable to you. The options don't have to be the same dollar value or size, but each should advance your company's business strategy as well as your *sales strategy for this customer*. And while every sales rep would love to do a multimillion-dollar deal with a new customer, most customers would rather "dip their toe in the water," starting off with a smaller deal that minimizes their risk. Wouldn't you be happy with a smaller deal that allows you to get your foot in the door and prove that you can provide value—one that opens that door to a much larger follow-on deal?

The title of each option should read as an outcome or value proposition that is meaningful to the customer. It should clearly explain what the option will deliver. As an example, Figure 2.3 represents the options that will be presented by Agile to MFS in the case story. (We'll go into greater detail later about their structure and strategy.) Note that in this example, labels like *good*, *better*, and *best* are replaced by detailed, informative labels that clearly communicate the differentiation among the options. It is important to present each option as acceptable to you, and the customer should feel free to pick the one that is right for them with no sense of one option being "better" than another.

Options for Moving Forward

	Complete Worldwide Integration Ahead of Schedule	Complete Worldwide and AIC Ahead of Schedule (at lowest cost)	Complete Worldwide and AIC Ahead of Schedule (plus future acquisitions)
Solution	Agile Dataccess cost: $13.68M	Agile Dataccess cost: $15.75M	Agile Dataccess cost: $17.77M
Schedule	5 weeks from contract signing	Worldwide: 5 weeks; AIC: 8 weeks from contract signing	Worldwide: 5 weeks, AIC: 8 weeks (future acquisition TBD)
Discount	31.6%	34.7%	38.3%
Implementation Services	15 Agile Service Engineers Cost: $920K	17 Agile Service Engineers Cost: $1.06M	17 Agile Service Engineers, 3 Agile Engineers on staff (3 years) Cost: $1.65M (yr 1), $590K (yrs 2-3)
Worldwide IT Staff Training	10 MFS IT staff onsite Cost: $80K	10 MFS IT staff onsite Cost: $80K	14 MFS IT staff onsite Cost: $112K
Platinum Support	Dedicated staff and call-in number 24/7 Cost: $240K annually	Dedicated staff and call-in number 24/7 Cost: $240K annually	Dedicated staff and call-in number 24/7 Cost: $240K annually
Contract Term	1 year	2 years	3 years
Software Maintenance	1 year	2 years	3 years
Payment Terms	100% up front	75% up front / 25% at completion of AIC integration	3 equal payments at the beginning of each year
Other Items	2 References, jointly present 1 Conference Paper	4 References, 2 Conference Papers, 1 Case Study	6 References, 3 Conference Papers, 2 Case Studies

Agile

Figure 2.3: Case Story (Agile to MFS) Options

It is a best practice to present the options side-by-side so that the customer can easily compare them. It is also best to stick to only the key deal levers (see Book II in this series) so that you can keep the options to a single page. Avoid using your terminology or acronyms—you want the options to be perfectly clear to the customer. In this case, Agile only uses "Dataccess," which is the name of their software platform. All other terminology is in the customer's language.

Options can be constructed around a variety of business criteria. One of the simplest is scope of work, where you present different deal sizes based on the volume and nature of the work you're proposing. Another way to construct options is around different business arrangements, such as "pay as you go," volume-tiered pricing, or a long-term, strategic contract. You can also build options around different levels of risk. No matter how you develop them, options must be relevant to *this* customer for *this* opportunity at *this* point in time. There is no "canned" template of options that will work every time.

Additionally, do not present these options as the *only ones* available to the customer. In most cases the final negotiated deal is a *combination of two or more of the options*, so you should present your options as simply three that you have developed based on what you believe may be important to the customer. Let them know that you are more than happy to consider other options they may come up with and that you will entertain changing any option to best meet their needs. This sends the clear message that you are flexible and that, beyond simply growing their options from one to three, you are inviting them to participate in the process of building an option that is good for both parties (see the sidebar below). Now, how different do you think you will look to the customer compared to a competitor that provides them with one option?

One of my clients has become truly masterful with the multiple acceptable options format. When presenting a compelling proposal, they bring the customer into their boardroom, where an overhead LCD projects onto a whiteboard. When they put the options up, they hand the customer a marker and ask them to go to the whiteboard and circle the option they like best. After the customer has made their selection, the seller asks, "How could this option be improved?" When the customer responds, the seller simply begins trading items in and out of the deal. The whole process only takes about an hour—and these are large, complicated deals. They take a picture of the marked up whiteboard and tell their customer that the next day they will have a formal written proposal and contract on their desk that includes everything they just discussed. Their customers love it! And why not? The final deal is "their deal," as they got to change it and make it work best for them. Some of their customers have even brought in their own CEOs to see the process in action. This is a great example of positive and powerful differentiation!

Finally, multiple acceptable options are most effective when they are *presented as early as possible in the sales cycle*. Once you have a reasonable idea of the outcomes important to the customer, the outlines of a great deal, and the alternative you are competing against, it is an ideal time to help the customer focus on the potential ways you could move the deal forward. When you allow the customer to participate in choosing the best way forward, you are in effect enabling them to *buy* (rather than just *pay for*) your solution. The deal they help construct is now "their deal"—one they will be highly motivated to close! This goes a long way toward shortening sales cycles.

We've established that the purpose of the proposal is to serve as a crucial bridge between the selling activities and the coming negotiation. We also addressed how to manage uncertainty and risk by using multiple acceptable options—one of the key objectives, and perhaps the heart, of your proposal.

Let's now turn our attention to the other critical objectives of a compelling proposal.

CHAPTER 3

The Objectives of a Compelling Proposal

*Trust, Credibility, and Making
It Easy to Choose You*

Many salespeople complain that selling is just plain harder now than it was in the past. Negotiations too. These days you are more likely to sell to customers who are better informed and more educated on the state of your business, the particulars of your offering, customers who buy and use your products and services, and the ups and downs of your industry. And they are just as well informed about your competitors. Of course, this is due in large part to the volumes of information freely available on the internet. Yet time and again I see the same, information-saturated salespeople fall back on the trusted and tired proposal formats they have always used, ones that do nothing more than regurgitate the *same publicly available information*. These salespeople offer little to no value to a customer trying to make an informed buying decision. In short, the current state of supplier proposals is truly abysmal.

Buying groups frequently engage me to review proposals from suppliers (sellers), but as I've written, nine times out of ten I know what the proposals are going to say before they hit my inbox. They focus almost exclusively on the supplier, their products and services, office locations, etc. This work has convinced me that most sellers *don't read their own proposals*. If you have not put yourself in your customer's shoes and tried to make it through one of your own, I highly recommend this exercise. In fact, bookmark this spot right now and go find one of your latest proposals. (You might want to put on a pot of coffee before you start.)

It is safe to say that most suppliers have marketing departments that can produce slick brochures and sophisticated graphics—and don't forget the TLAs (three-letter acronyms). The problem is that the role of marketing is to *produce leads* that may eventually turn into opportunities. But if you are submitting a proposal to a qualified *live* opportunity, then ask yourself these questions:

→ How relevant is your marketing messaging to the customer at this juncture?

→ How many customers speak your language and understand (much less care) what your acronyms mean?

→ Are you really making it easier for the customer to choose your company when your proposal is all about you?

→ If you and your competitors are doing the same thing, then how different do you really look?

The upshot is that when everybody looks the same, more often than not the final decision will come down to *price*. And why not? This is the path that you (and your competitors) have paved for the buyer, and if price is the only meaningful differentiator, then it is certainly their safest choice.

If you want your customer to trust you, show them what you know about *their business*, not yours. They expect you to understand your industry, your products, and your services, but they won't trust you until they believe you understand *them* and what they want to accomplish. What is ultimately most important to your customer is what you are uniquely positioned provide: a best-fit solution that is clearly tied to their business, their needs, and their goals. (This is why the "death of the B2B salesperson" is greatly exaggerated.[1])

---

1   This Forbes article is a good (and brief) entrée to the topic. http://www.forbes.com/sites/forrester/2015/04/15/death-of-a-b2b-salesman/

Much research has been done in the past twenty years on what makes a customer choose and remain loyal to a supplier, and the findings of this research are surprisingly consistent. Based on recent studies[2], a little less than half of the decision is based on a combination of technology, company brand, service and support, and *price*. Surprised? The remainder can be divided roughly between your credibility and/or trustworthiness and how easy you make it for a customer to choose you. Perhaps *not* surprisingly, my experience has shown that this is where most deals are lost.

We've just covered managing uncertainty as one of the objectives of a compelling proposal. Let's now delve into reinforcing trust, establishing credibility, and making it easier to buy from you.

REINFORCING TRUST AND ESTABLISHING CREDIBILITY

What makes a customer trust you? Two things.

First, trust is built on a history of both delivering value and getting credit for that value. That is, your customer has purchased from you, you have delivered value, *and* they have given you credit for delivering value. I call this

2   Based on research by The CEB Sales Leadership Council (https://www.cebglobal.com/exbd/ sales-service/sales/index.page?) and Forrester Q4 2016 North American And European Buyer Expectations of Sales Interactions Online Survey.

past value delivered (PVD), and it is the subject of the final book in this series. At first glance, you may find this idea simplistic, but let's test it with a few questions, in ascending order of difficulty.

Thinking about one of your largest accounts, how long have they been a customer? You should be able to answer this readily. Now, how much have they bought from your company in the past three years? With a little work, you can come up with that number. Finally, what value have you and your company delivered to that customer? This one's not so simple because, believe it or not, the answer to this question is different from the answer to the one before it. That is, the quantity of goods or services they bought from you is almost certainly not the same as the value you have delivered. But what if you *do* know the difference and can answer this question. If so, you get a bonus question: *Has the customer given you credit for delivering that value?*

Think about it for a minute. If you are not sure of the value you and your company have delivered to a customer, what are the odds that *they* know? The hard fact is, they don't. I can assure you that this is a troubling question (for you), that is being asked by more and more buying organizations. Someone internally is looking at the total spend over time with your company and asking, *what are we getting for it?* If no one knows the answer, you now have a big target on your back. At the very least, the customer will assume they have been over-paying for your products or services, and you can plan on some tough, *price-only* negotiations in the future!

The second reason a customer will trust you is because of what you know about them right now. You know the details of their business, the opportunities they are pursuing, and the business problems they are trying to solve. Additionally, you understand the outcomes they are trying to achieve and how they will measure success— and they believe you are focused on helping them achieve those outcomes. Contrary to a popular sales myth, that "it's all about the relationship," your customer is not looking for more friends. If so, I recommend buying them a dog. What they really need is suppliers they can trust. The relationship happens *after* the value has been delivered, not before.

What about credibility, and how is it different from trust? Many sales reps confuse these two concepts, which is understandable as they are related but meaningfully distinct. As stated above, customers trust you because of what you know about them and what they are trying to accomplish right now. Credibility, on the other hand, is established when you've "been there and done that." For instance, if you are trying to sell *more of something* to an existing customer, you will have credibility with them if you delivered value the first time(s) you sold that thing to them. But what if you are trying to sell something *new* to that customer? Now you establish credibility by demonstrating that your company has solved similar problems and delivered similar desired outcomes to other customers. References play a big role here, which we will cover when we discuss past value delivered in the next chapter.

MAKE IT EASY TO CHOOSE YOU

How do you make it easy for a customer to choose you and your company?

Start by giving them an irresistible value proposition, one that makes them want to do a deal and do it right now. Then give the customer options so that they can participate in choosing to buy what is best for them and not feel that you are trying to *sell them what you want them to buy*. It's no more complicated than that.

These concepts are simple. But echoing a precept from earlier in the series, that doesn't mean they are easy (which may be why I see so few selling organizations embrace them). That's good news for you because *how* you sell, *how* you propose, and *how* you negotiate a deal are ultimately as important to the customer as *what* you are selling, perhaps more so. If closing deals were just about the latest technology, robust services, and a reasonable price, your job would be replaced by an online catalog. This is why your company needs a salesforce! Remember, if you think selling complex deals is challenging, it is even more challenging for the customer to make an informed, complex decision—one they can feel comfortable is the best decision for them.

Your role is to make it easy for the customer to choose you and your firm by building trust and credibility while managing any uncertainty surrounding the deal. These are the things that customers value most when making a decision. Lucky for you, they're almost impossible to "Google."

PRESENTATION OR WRITTEN PROPOSAL?

The compelling proposal format can be delivered as a concise (and short) written document or a seven-slide presentation. In either case, your primary objective is to get in front of all the key buying influencers to have a dialogue. This is always preferable to sending a thick, formal proposal, which, except for the executive summary and the pricing page, probably won't be read—at least not by the key decision makers.

Let's face it: we are sales reps, not Shakespeare. Presentations and live meetings are a chance to get in front of key decision makers and have a meaningful *dialogue*, a word I stress because it is critical. Key decision makers, especially senior management, have told me time and again that they don't want to sit and watch another one-sided presentation, no matter how slick. These people hold the keys to the kingdom, and you are likely to learn more by having a conversation with them than during the entire sales cycle up to that point. Aside from getting answers to your questions, you will also make a positive and lasting impression on the customer simply by *asking thoughtful questions* during the dialogue. Finally, you will set up the right negotiation, which you may be able to complete during the presentation itself! (It happens more often than you may think.)

Now that we've explored the objectives of a compelling proposal, it's time to look at the components of this seven-page document.

CHAPTER 4

The Components of a Compelling Proposal

Hit the Objectives Head-On

The seven pages (or slides) of your compelling proposal should be built around five straightforward objectives (detailed in Figure 4.1): to reinforce trust, set up the right negotiation, establish credibility, manage uncertainty, and make it easy for your customer to *buy from* you. You can think of the proposal itself as a kind of story, one about how you are uniquely suited to help your customer achieve the outcomes that are important to them. The story is a journey (or discovery), one that the customer is undertaking to reach a better, more prosperous destination than where they are now. You know exactly where they want to go, you've scouted the territory ahead (done your research), and using *their language* (not yours), you explain to them how your solution will help them reach their destination on the straightest possible path. In short, this story mirrors their buying process.

COMPELLING PROPOSAL PRESENTATION
Objectives of a Compelling Proposal

- Reinforce **Trust**
- Set up the **"Right Negotiation"**
- Establish **Credibility**
- Manage the **Uncertainty** that's inherent in any complex B2B deal
- Make it easier for the Customer to **Buy** (and know it was the right choice for them)

Present as *early as possible* in the Sales Cycle

Figure 4.1: Objectives of a Compelling Proposal

Whatever narrative you choose, keeping your "story" grounded in these simple but powerful objectives will greatly increase your odds of success. I have found that they work for deals both small and large. After all, small customers buy for the same reasons as large ones—they just buy in smaller quantities—and both are trying to make the right decisions for themselves and their businesses. Note that your proposal should be in a bullet format on each page; this will help facilitate productive dialogue with the customer.

Now have a look at the template for the compelling proposal in Figure 4.2, showing how you will accomplish all these objectives.

MANAGING UNCERTAINTY AND PROPOSING OUTCOMES
Compelling Proposal Presentation Template

	1. Cover Slide – overall Value Proposition
Trust and Set Up Right Negotiation	2. Validate the desired Outcomes the Customer is looking to achieve
	3. Translate those Outcomes into the key Deal Levers for the Customer
	4. Share what is Important to us in a Deal
	5. Present Past Value Delivered to increase the risk of their Alternative
Credibility and Easier to Buy	6. Provide Multiple Acceptable Options to *Manage Uncertainty*
	7. Summary (rephrase slide #2)

Figure 4.2: Compelling Proposal Template

I'm often asked: When is the ideal time to present the proposal? The answer: as early in the sales cycle as possible. Once you have a good handle on what is important to the customer in terms of outcomes, timeline, and success criteria, this is an ideal time to present it. I'm also asked: Who is the ideal audience for the proposal? All key decision makers, if possible (see the sidebar).

One word of caution. The compelling proposal format is designed to resonate with the key decision makers (those who own the outcomes and need to make a decision), rather than technical influencers. If you try this format with the latter, it will likely fail. Why? Key decision makers are concerned with business outcomes and results. That's their primary focus—what they are paid to produce—and it's what a compelling proposal is about. Technical influencers are more concerned with processes and deliverables (think projects), and while the business focus of a compelling proposal won't be lost on them, it is neither "where they live" nor where they generally do their best thinking.

This does not mean that technical influencers and evaluators are unimportant to winning a deal. Obviously, you must sell to them by demonstrating the technical merits of your offering, especially considering that key decision makers will likely turn to them to validate the technical aspects of your offer.

A NOTE ON TECHNICAL PROPOSALS (OR TECHNICAL CONTENT IN COMPELLING PROPOSALS)

If you are selling something technical or complex (or both), it is normal for your proposal to include additional materials detailing technical aspects of your product or solution. It is perfectly fine to include these in an addendum or appendix; however, in my experience they are rarely needed. Here we will focus on the *business and outcomes* aspects of the compelling proposal.

This is not to minimize the importance of the technical sale. In many cases if you do not clear performance hurdles or meet minimum technical specifications, you will not "pass go" and could be excluded from consideration. But I have found that technical decision makers are rarely empowered to approve a deal or write a check. More often than not, they establish minimum requirement hurdles and can make thumbs-up or thumbs-down judgments based on technical requirements and specifications. Here, we will assume that you and your team can clear such hurdles and have validated that any technical requirements *support the customer's desired outcomes*. If they don't, the technical evaluators will not be aligned with the business decision makers—something I see with surprising frequency.

Now, let's take a break from putting together *your* compelling proposal and return to our case story to learn how Paul and the team will tackle *theirs*!

Case Story Continued

CAST OF CHARACTERS—RECAP

1. *Paul Stockard, Agile Sales Rep:* Paul is the sales rep for Agile Information Solutions (Agile) and has been calling on Worldwide Financial Solutions, Inc. (Worldwide) for the past five months.

2. *Jane Jones, Agile Sales Engineer:* Jane handles all the technical aspects of an opportunity and manages proof-of-concept tests with a customer prior to a sale. She also supports the customer after the sale.

3. *Douglas Hand, Agile Lead Engineer for Services and Support:* Doug is responsible for implementation after the sale as well as customer support. If Agile is chosen, he and his team will lead the integration project.

4. *Jared Carlisle, Agile Senior Financial Analyst:* Jared's job is to ensure that any Agile offering will be profitable to the company as well as in line with deals

given to other customers. He also helps account teams quantify the value they expect to deliver to customers.

5. **Caroline Borders,** *Agile VP of Legal:* Caroline is an experienced attorney who is savvy in the technology industry and handles most legal negotiations of contracts, terms, and conditions with customers.

6. **Tim Rosser,** *Agile VP of Sales:* Tim is an experienced IT sales executive who is known to be unflappable as well as a great coach and mentor. Paul and his team have a very good relationship with Tim.

7. **Susan Renly,** *Worldwide Chief Information Officer (CIO):* Susan has been a long-time supporter of Agile and Paul. The recent acquisition of Worldwide by Mega Financial Services (MFS) has created a terrific career opportunity for her as she is in the running for the position of CIO of MFS. (The current CIO recently left the company.) This would be a significant jump in responsibility and pay and seems contingent on the successful integration of Worldwide into MFS.

8. **Kenneth Beckley,** *Former CEO of Worldwide:* Kenneth is a supporter of the cloud-based approach used by Agile and has been named to the MFS board of directors as part of the acquisition. His first assignment is to ensure that the MFS salesforce has access to Worldwide's applications and data.

9. **Bill Sellers,** *MFS SVP of Operations:* Bill heads up the steering committee and has been charged by the

MFS board of directors with the completion of the Worldwide IT integration in less than four months. It appears he has been given significant incentives to do so, as he is anxious to get the integration underway. Paul has met Bill several times and he appears to be a supporter.

10. *Jack Grossman, MFS VP of Technology:* Also on the steering committee, Jack's role is to determine the integration approach. Jack is rumored to be in the running for the newly open MFS CIO position. He is a big supporter of JCN, the primary competition for the opportunity, so Paul does not expect him to be an advocate for Agile or their approach.

11. *Stephanie Holder, MFS Senior Procurement Manager:* MFS has a reputation as a very tough negotiator, and Stephanie is a big reason for that. It also appears that the procurement department wields a lot of influence and power at MFS.

When Paul and the account team learned that JCN was offering to do the Worldwide integration by giving away their competing software and services—absolutely free— it was hardly good news, but it confirmed that MFS's clear alternative was JCN. As a result, Paul and his team took a big step back and analyzed the alternative that Agile was competing against. They knew that they couldn't afford to fall into the trap of competing head-to-head with JCN on their terms. They needed to carefully qualify the opportunity for Agile and, if it passed muster, determine how they were going to win it.

Sixteen million in savings out of the box would be a strong opener for JCN, but the savings would be more than offset by the cost of their proprietary hardware. What's more, their installation timeline—at least two months beyond the board's deadline—would be a big negative. MFS, after all, would have to consider the cost, both in stock value and reputation, of missing market expectations in the event of a delayed integration, with implications that would go all the way to the CEO. Paul was betting that Bill Sellers would not risk choosing a vendor that would almost certainly go over the all-important deadline, and he knew that Bill had been given strong incentives to ensure that didn't happen!

But despite all the tangible and intangible costs and risks of choosing JCN for this project, MFS would think long and hard before putting their long-term relationship with such a strategically important supplier at risk. For their part, JCN was already playing hardball. Behind the scenes, they had succeeded in convincing MFS's CEO to move the presentation date up to this Friday. Now Paul and the team had fewer than three days to prepare Agile's proposal presentation for the steering committee. To make matters worse, MFS had just announced that they were acquiring American Investment Corporation

(AIC), a niche player who completely outsourced their IT function to JCN.

In a productive meeting with Bill Sellers and Susan Renly, Paul had validated the outcomes that were important to MFS. He left the meeting certain that Susan was a strong supporter and sponsor of Agile, and he had begun to believe that Bill was leaning Agile's way. He and the team had done their homework, and with Susan's help, his value proposition crisply answered why Bill and MFS should care. It also clearly laid out Agile's incremental value and exactly what they would deliver.

Of course, the answer to the question, *why now?* could not have been more obvious: time was of the essence, and only Agile could bring a successful solution to bear within the board's time frame. Everything would hinge on the compelling proposal the Agile team would present this Friday and how good Paul and his team made Bill look to the board and CEO.

* * *

Susan called Paul shortly after their meeting with Bill, this time to get the ball rolling in earnest.

"Paul, I'd like you and your team to be prepared to present your proposal this Friday at 10 a.m. As a reminder, you'll be presenting to the entire steering committee. JCN goes on at eight, and each of you will have ninety minutes."

"Sounds great," Paul responded. "Of course we will be there, and I really appreciate the opportunity, Susan. But I have a few questions for you, if I may."

"Fire away," she replied.

"First, when will we have the technical details on the AIC acquisition?" Paul asked.

"I just checked with my team, and Jane should have received everything by now. If you need anything else," she added, "please let us know."

"Oh, we will!" Paul laughed, though there was nothing funny about the latest news regarding MFS's acquisition of AIC. Thank goodness Susan and her team were on the ball and able to get the critical specs to Agile so quickly.

He then inquired, "Has Bill been able to validate whether MFS will require *all* of the Worldwide data and applications, or is there some sort of priority ranking?"

"Timely question," she chuckled. "Bill just sent me a text saying that MFS will require all of the Worldwide data and applications to be integrated. You must have made quite an impression on him as I did not expect to hear back on this question for another day or so."

"A *positive* impression, I hope!" Paul exclaimed.

Susan shared a few more thoughts about how Agile and her team might handle the AIC acquisition. She batted some ideas back and forth with Paul, and they agreed on an approach that would almost certainly catch JCN off guard—and hopefully impress the rest of the MFS steering committee.

Are there any more surprises? Paul wondered as he hung up the phone.

* * *

Early the next morning, Paul pulled his team together to lay out a plan of attack.

"Good morning everyone! We don't have a lot of time this morning, so while you're working on your second cup, I want to jump right in. The biggest issue in this deal is that JCN is charging the same for their software and services as what you paid for your breakroom coffee: zero!"

A mix of smiles, furrowed brows, and puzzled looks told

Paul that he needed to take a moment and let this point sink in.

"I know, I know, that's about what this stuff we call coffee is worth," he continued. "But kidding aside, JCN is trying to take charge and frame this sale and future negotiation around price. *We're not going to take that bait.* We're going to make this deal about *time.*"

He explained that Agile's strategy would be to change the game and make the deal about meeting or beating the timeline put in place by the MFS board. "MFS hasn't said word one about the value of free stuff, but they've made it very clear that their deadline is sacrosanct. This gives us an opportunity to reframe the discussion, at least in part, around the value we bring by significantly beating that deadline."

"But our strategy will also be about enabling future growth. Our value proposition will demonstrate to MFS how our solution will facilitate that growth through further acquisitions."

Paul went on to review how the objectives of the proposal presentation would drive the format of the presentation—and the meeting—and that the format should also drive a dialogue. At this point they had as many questions as answers, and they needed to:

→ Present Agile's overall value proposition to MFS.

→ Validate what was important to MFS (the outcomes) and what they were trying to achieve, and frame the sale and the negotiation in Agile's favor.

→ Frame the sale and right negotiation by connecting the dots between the desired outcomes and the deal levers that would be important to MFS in the deal.

→ Present what was important to Agile in the deal to further frame the sale and the negotiation.

→ Present the past value delivered by Agile to increase the risk to MFS should they turn to JCN.

→ Give MFS options to consider for moving forward.

→ Summarize everything.

"Alright, we need to wrap this up," Paul continued, "but I also need to be sure you have enough information about the AIC acquisition to offer an option for that integration too." He paused to survey the room. "Any comments or questions? Jane, how did the numbers look from the technical specs Susan sent you?"

"My team and I crunched the numbers," Jane replied, "and we feel that, working with the Worldwide team, we can manage the demands of the integration, storage, software, and support services."

Doug Hand, the lead engineer for services and support, was less sanguine.

"Paul, I'm sorry," Doug interjected, "but I still need some convincing on this approach. I see the advantage of shifting the focus from price to time, but JCN is putting a huge giveaway on the table. I just don't see how we can counter that." He went on to argue that cost was always a big consideration when dealing with IT organizations, and in his experience it was often the deciding issue.

Paul acknowledged Doug and agreed that this wasn't exactly going to be slow-pitch softball, but focusing on the board's timeline was the best chance they had. For now, though, he needed to keep things moving and shift the team's attention to the options they would present.

"We need to present three viable options to MFS," he said, turning to a flipchart he'd sketched up. "And just to be clear, there are no red-herrings or throwaways here. This is not a trick, and we can't risk putting a known loser on this list to steer a customer to options that are better for us. As soon as we do that, you can bet that's *exactly* the one they'll pick!"

Paul knew he was preaching to the choir, but he felt it worth repeating that every option should be good for both sides. With that out of the way, he talked the team through the flipchart:

- → Option #1: WFSI integration under schedule (stand-alone)
- → Option #2: WFSI and AIC integration (reducing schedule and integration costs)
- → Option #3: WFSI and AIC integration as well as flexibility for further growth through future acquisitions

Everyone agreed that the options made sense, at least based on what they knew at that time. In any case, every time they had done this in the past, the final deals were almost always a combination of one or more options, rarely a single, verbatim, line-item option. The point of this list was to give everyone in the sale and subsequent negotiation a good place to start. But the real power of the options was in the collaboration they inspired, and the sense of ownership of the final deal the process created for the customer.

With that settled, Paul put the team to work pulling together a compelling seven-slide, outcome-based proposal presentation. Detailed schedules, technology overviews, etc. would be attached as appendix slides if they were needed during the presentation, though Paul had found that was rarely the case. After numerous reviews, revisions, and phone calls with Agile sales management, operations, and finance, the final presentation was completed late in the evening.

* * *

Let's take a break from the case story and review the proposal presentation that Paul and his team pulled together to gain a detailed understanding of the components of a compelling proposal.

Integrate the Worldwide
Acquisition Ahead of Schedule
and the AIC Acquisition Quickly
at the Lowest Cost

. . . . Ag*i*le

COVER PAGE OR TITLE SLIDE

A couple of quick thoughts on the cover page of your proposal: This slide must clearly communicate to the customer what the entire proposal is about. Too often I see cover pages or title slides with indecipherable acronyms listing products or services. These may be the "language" of the seller, but to the buyer they are Greek. The title of your proposal should be your value proposition, and it should be straightforward and easy to understand. It should tell the customer what you intend to deliver, how it is uniquely different from their alternative(s), and why they should care.

For example, in the title slide above, Agile clearly lists two integrations as the deliverable, Worldwide and AIC. They differentiate their offer by promising the Worldwide integration ahead of the board's schedule, and the AIC integration quickly and at a lower cost. The decision makers should care because they have already stated that these criteria are important to them. If you follow these guidelines, your cover page will make you stand out, and, importantly, it will telegraph early in the presentation that you understand the customer's needs and intend to be direct and clear in your communication.

MFS's Objectives

- Complete Worldwide integration by Board's deadline or sooner
- Provide MFS Sales access to all Worldwide data and applications
- Minimize disruption to current MFS IT operations
- Minimize downtime after implementation
- Complete within budget
- Complete AIC integration as quickly as possible and minimize costs
- Create technology solutions and capabilities to enable future acquisitions

. . . . Ag*i*le

CUSTOMER OUTCOMES

To keep things simple (which is how most customers like it), build your proposal format based on the customer's outcomes. Begin with a summary to validate the outcomes they want to achieve. Remember, they aren't *buying* products and solutions—that is what they are *paying for*—they are buying a new (and hopefully improved) set of outcomes. They are trying to solve a business problem or capitalize on business opportunities, and they typically want to do this within a certain timeframe.

Start your compelling proposal with this section because it sends the message that you are focused on the buyer's needs and haven't lost sight of the outcomes they are trying to achieve. Remember to present this list humbly rather than acting as if it were fact; you are here to validate the list, not deliver it. After listing the customer outcomes, be sure to include a request for confirmation that the list was correctly captured. Was something missed or has anything changed? This sets up a powerful dialogue that creates the tone for the remainder of the presentation. It also reinforces that you are focused on the customer's outcomes, not the products or services being sold, and it frames the sale and the subsequent negotiation. In short, you are making it all about their desired outcomes, not your solution.

Key Elements of Our Offer

- Agile Dataccess Platform
- Experienced Program Manager
- Platinum Support
- Implementation Services
- Platform Training for MFS Staff
- Close within 2 Weeks

MFS Key Outcomes

- Worldwide Integration Deadline
- Access to all Worldwide Data
- Minimize Disruption to MFS IT
- Zero Downtime
- Complete Within Budget
- AIC Integration Schedule/Costs
- Enable Future Acquisitions

. . . . **Ag*i*le**

WHAT IS IMPORTANT TO THE CUSTOMER IN YOUR DEAL

This section covers one of the most important steps in selling, yet one I find missing or absent from too many proposals and selling processes. After you have confirmed your customer's outcomes, you must help them *translate those outcomes* into the key deal levers that will be important to them in the deal. You want them to confirm what a great deal looks like to them. For example, let's assume that time is of the essence and your customer is short on staff to implement or install your solution. In this case, one item that should be important to them is a start date that will meet their deadline. They are also likely to value implementation support that will help them make their schedule. The start date of the project will depend on the date you close this deal. Now you are making the *close date of the deal* important to the customer and not just to you. In essence, they now "own" this date along with you, significantly reducing the odds of "deal slippage" past quarter end.

Your objective here is to further shape the sale and what it is about while framing the subsequent negotiation. The customer will be acknowledging that there is *more on the table than price*. Other things are important as well. For instance, in the case story, note how the close date is linked to meeting or exceeding the board's deadline. Again, ask for confirmation that you have correctly surmised what should be in a deal in order to achieve your customer's outcomes. "Is this list right? Did we miss anything?" When the key buying influencers are in the room, this can spark different individuals to share what is important to them. If all were not aligned walking into the presentation, this becomes an opportunity to help them get aligned. After all, you are doing a single deal with your customer, not one deal with operations, another with IT, and yet another with procurement!

But don't just validate the correct items, make sure you learn the importance of each item to the customer so that you can help them prioritize these items. This will give you a much clearer picture of what a great deal looks like to your customer and thus the target you want to hit. It will also get them to start thinking about the final deal in terms of what is most important to them. Experience has shown me that most customers have *not* thought about this, and the salesperson who helps them gain this understanding brings tremendous value!

What Is Important to Agile in this Deal

1. Worldwide storage and software (Dataccess) discount
2. Adequate level of Implementation Services to meet deadline
3. Training for minimum 10 MFS IT staff
4. Deal close in two weeks to meet Board deadline
5. Appropriate level of support after implementation
6. Payment up front
7. Contract term (longer is better)
8. Quarterly Customer Value Reviews with SVP and CIO
9. Storage, software, and support for AIC acquisition
10. Public awareness (references, co-publish papers, conferences)

. . . . **Ag*i*le**

WHAT IS IMPORTANT TO YOU IN THIS DEAL

Perhaps the most controversial section of the proposal—at least for most of my clients—is when you share with your customer what is important to you in the deal. The objective is to further shape the sale and frame the negotiation (it's not about any single item) as well as to educate the customer about what you and your organization want out of the deal. You might not think that your customer would care about what is important to you in a deal, but you'd be surprised by how much time buying organizations spend trying to discern where sellers are coming from. In fact, I'm willing to bet that you currently have customers who want to do a deal that is good for both organizations, but they can't do this without an understanding of what's important to your company.

A lot of salespeople feel very uncomfortable with this concept because of the way they have been trained to negotiate. Sellers believe that sharing what's important to them gives the customer power in the negotiation. Let me reassure you this is not the case. Power is a function of alternatives to doing a deal, as we learned in the previous book. When you tell your customer what is important to you in a deal, *you are not giving them power over you in the negotiation*. Instead, you are *empowering them to help you craft a deal* that works for both sides. Don't make them work for this information!

If you remain unconvinced of the effectiveness of sharing what is important to you in a deal, let's test this approach—and your reservations—with a scenario. In this scenario, you are the buyer and I am the seller. I already know that you need to buy a solution from someone, so doing nothing is not an option for you. I share with you that closing a deal before the end of the quarter is very important to me. I also explain that as a publicly traded company, Wall Street naturally expects us to deliver on our projected quarterly sales figures. Using your tactical negotiation training as a buyer, you tell me that you're not really ready to do a deal or interested in closing one before next quarter.

My response is simple: that's fine, but we have plenty of business lined up for next quarter, and thus my sales management will not be willing to offer as generous a discount at that time. You also mentioned that free training and implementation support is an important component of the deal to you, and we will not be in a position to offer that next quarter or the foreseeable future as our teams are completely booked then.

So how have you used what's important to me (my preferred timeline) against me? You haven't. I let you know that since the delayed deal was not as good for us, I would not be in a position to give you everything you wanted next quarter or beyond. Obviously, it's important that I also have alignment with my management and that we are prepared to stand by that statement!

When my clients use this approach, their results are overwhelmingly positive. They often hear their customers proclaim that they would rather do business with a company that knows where they are going and what is important to them. Or customers will say that this is the first time a seller has shared this information with them, and it makes them believe they are dealing with an organization that is truly interested in a long-term partnership.

I hope you will consider adding this important section to your proposal. If you do let the customer know what a good deal looks like to you, it's worth noting that they may not always like what you have to say. And sometimes they simply won't care. But if you handle this conversation skillfully, you can make them care. I've also found that the best deals—the ones that have the most potential to foster long-term, mutually beneficial relationships—are grounded in common terms that create a strategic foundation for a win/win negotiation and, ultimately, delivering the value the customer wants.

Past Value Delivered by Agile

- Completed Global Financial Solutions integration for Worldwide in five weeks—three weeks ahead of schedule
- Completed International Assets Corp. integration for Worldwide in three weeks—six weeks ahead of schedule
- Completed integration of Smith Financial Planning and Jones Investments merger within one month—two months ahead of schedule
- Completed two simultaneous acquisitions for Signet Investments three months ahead of schedule, eliminating need for new hardware

. . . . Ag*i*le

PAST VALUE DELIVERED

In this section of the proposal, you remind an existing customer of the past value you've delivered to them. This information should be readily available if you have been selling value and following up *after the sale* to ensure that you and your organization delivered that value by measuring the outcomes the customer was looking for. The most effective way to validate past value delivered is through customer value reviews (CVRs). Conducting these regular reviews with the customer will increase the risk of any alternative they may be considering. If your company has a proven track record of delivering value to a particular customer, why would they take the risk of going with a competitor? For most businesses there are substantial costs and risk associated with switching suppliers, and such a disruptive move would only be contemplated when the alternative presents decidedly more value.

We will cover CVRs in greater detail in the final book in this series, *Can't-Lose Accounts*. For now, just know that these meetings with the customer's key decision makers begin after you have made the sale and after they have implemented your solution. The primary objective of the customer value review is to ensure that you have delivered the value they were expecting and to *get credit for delivering that value*. This solidifies your position with and relevance to the customer, and it increases their perceived risk of going with a competitor. Another benefit of the CVR worth noting is the opportunity it provides to remediate any shortfalls in delivering the promised value, and that such a stance is itself valuable to key decision makers. Almost everyone understands that complex solutions will have issues. What customers want is a supplier who will proactively identify and address those issues.

If you are not selling to an existing customer, provide examples where the outcomes you delivered for other customers were *similar* to those sought by the potential new customer. Briefly share the business problem, how you helped solve it, and the results you delivered. This will increase both your credibility and the risk of any alternative under consideration.

Many sales organizations make the mistake of focusing first on examples (or references) from the customer's industry. However, if the problems you solved are not related to what this customer is trying to achieve, then such examples are of little merit. Instead, focus first on providing examples of customers that had the same *business problem or desired outcomes*. Only then turn your attention to those that may be in the same or a similar industry.

	Complete Worldwide Integration Ahead of Schedule	Complete Worldwide and AIC Ahead of Schedule (at lowest cost)	Complete Worldwide and AIC Ahead of Schedule (plus future acquisitions)
Solution	Agile Dataccess cost: $13.68M	Agile Dataccess cost: $15.75M	Agile Dataccess cost: $17.77M
Schedule	5 weeks from contract signing	Worldwide: 5 weeks; AIC: 8 weeks from contract signing	Worldwide: 5 weeks, AIC: 8 weeks (future acquisition TBD)
Discount	31.6%	34.7%	38.3%
Implementation Services	15 Agile Service Engineers Cost: $920K	17 Agile Service Engineers Cost: $1.06M	17 Agile Service Engineers, 3 Agile Engineers on staff (3 years) Cost: $1.65M (yr 1), $590K (yrs 2-3)
Worldwide IT Staff Training	10 MFS IT staff onsite Cost: $80K	10 MFS IT staff onsite Cost: $80K	14 MFS IT staff onsite Cost: $112K
Platinum Support	Dedicated staff and call-in number 24/7 Cost: $240K annually	Dedicated staff and call-in number 24/7 Cost: $240K annually	Dedicated staff and call-in number 24/7 Cost: $240K annually
Contract Term	1 year	2 years	3 years
Software Maintenance	1 year	2 years	3 years
Payment Terms	100% up front	75% up front / 25% at completion of AIC integration	3 equal payments at the beginning of each year
Other Items	2 References, jointly present 1 Conference Paper	4 References, 2 Conference Papers, 1 Case Study	6 References, 3 Conference Papers, 2 Case Studies

Ag*i*le

OPTIONS FOR MOVING FORWARD

Options are the heart of the compelling proposal. Presenting options helps you manage the uncertainty inherent in the real world and increases the odds of success. Even more important, options enable the customer to *buy from you* rather than have a solution *sold to them*. They shape the sale and prevent single-issue negotiations (typically price) because each option is presented as a bundled offer. Each bundled offer contains a list of the products and services you are offering as well as quantities. It also includes items such as payment terms, guarantees (if any), support after the sale, key terms and conditions, etc.

There is a price attached to each option, but price is always a function of other terms, conditions, and items built into the bundle. Multiple acceptable options also enable you to better manage negotiation tactics that customers typically employ, like countering strictly on price. Finally, when a customer chooses or gravitates to one of the options, they reveal what is actually important to them. Any games being played during the sale are now over as the customer has shown their hand.

It bears repeating: do not present these options as the only ones available to the customer. In most cases, the final negotiated deal is a combination of two or more of the options. Present your options as simply three that you have developed based on what you believe to be important to the customer, and let them know that you are more than happy to consider other options they may come up with or entertain changing any option to best meet their needs. This sends the clear message that you are flexible and that the customer can choose or tailor the option that best suits them. How different do you think you will look to the customer compared to a competitor that provides them with only one option?

Our goal was to provide MFS solutions to...

- Complete Worldwide integration ahead of deadline
- Provide MFS Sales access to all Worldwide data and applications
- Minimize disruption to current MFS IT staff
- Maximize uptime after implementation
- Complete all work under MFS budget
- Complete AIC integration ahead of schedule at lowest cost
- Provide technology solutions to enable future acquisitions

. . . . Ag*i*le

SUMMARY AND APPENDICES OR ADDENDUMS

The last section of the proposal is simply a rewording of the second slide, recapping what is important to the customer and what you have tried to help them achieve. This closes the loop and reminds the customer why they are considering the proposal and what you are trying to deliver to them.

Please note that you can find a complete copy of Agile's compelling proposal in the Appendix.

* * *

Now, take a step back and look at the overall format of the compelling proposal template and how it flows. As I mentioned, it can be used for deals ranging from thousands to billions of dollars. (Of course, big deals come with big technical proposal addenda.) One significant advantage of this straightforward approach is that it distills the essence of the proposal and options into an easily digestible format. It is especially ideal when presenting to key decision makers, as it saves them the time of reading through a long proposal document. When delivered as a presentation, it allows them to discuss key points and ask questions along the way. After all, they got to be key decision makers because they like to ask questions and make tough decisions!

Finally, the compelling proposal is focused on the customer, the outcomes they are trying to achieve, the deal levers that will best enable them to achieve those results, and options for moving forward. What customer would not like that? Only two sections are about you: *What Is Important to You in this Deal* and the *Past Value Delivered* by you to this customer or customers with similar challenges and opportunities.

You've now done everything in your power to ensure you are making the *right sale,* selling the *right way,* and preparing for the *right negotiation.* In addition, you have managed the uncertainty that is always present in the real world by presenting the customer with options. Finally, you have managed to stand out and look "outstandingly" different to your customer!

Let's see how these concepts play out in the conclusion of our case story. We've just reviewed the proposal presentation slides. How will they work in an "actual" outcome-based, compelling proposal presentation?

CHAPTER 5

Case Story Conclusion

At the end of what seemed like one of the longest days of Paul's career, he was exhausted and anxious about the presentation. But he was satisfied that his team had done everything they could to prepare, at least under the circumstances. Now, with himself as the presenter, he needed to set the rest of the lineup for the presentation. Any questions of a technical nature would be handled by Jane, his sales engineer. Doug Hand, the lead engineer for services and support, would be present to meet and talk with the people who would be managing the integration, something Paul had found customers really appreciated. Finally, Paul had received an email from his VP of sales, Tim Rosser, saying he'd be attending the proposal presentation. Paul was pleased that Agile would be "showing the flag" with a senior executive in attendance, but the news didn't do much to ease the pressure he was feeling!

The night before the presentation, Paul struggled to sleep, catching at best a handful of fitful naps until he finally threw in the towel around 4:30. "Might as well use the time productively," he muttered on the way to the coffee pot. As the caffeine cut through the fog, he reviewed the presentation one last time. The key to success today was to get the MFS steering committee engaged and talking as much as possible during his team's ninety minutes. JCN would go before Agile, and Paul expected them to give the usual "dog and pony show," albeit an impressive one. But he wanted everything about Agile's presentation to look and feel different. There were many things he and his team needed to know, in particular whether MFS had thought through everything that was important to them in the deal. This was their only opportunity to get that information—and dialogue was key.

Finally, suited up and energized by nerves and coffee, Paul met Tim and the team at MFS headquarters thirty minutes before showtime. To groans of good-natured resignation, he reminded the team—one last time—of the objectives for the presentation.

"I really appreciate the care and preparation you've all put into this," he said. "Just remember, we're going to be more than a little 'out-of-the-box' today, and we can expect some interesting reactions from both MFS and the competition."

"Let's just hope 'interesting' means 'good'!" Jane interjected. Everyone chuckled in agreement, but they all seemed prepared and the mood was cautiously optimistic.

At 10:00 a.m. on the nose, Paul and his team were escorted into a large conference room dominated by an imposing mahogany table. As they made their way to the table, Susan stood and approached them warmly. "Paul, welcome to MFS!" she said. "It's my pleasure to introduce you to the MFS steering committee: Bill Sellers, SVP of operations—I believe you've met—Stephanie Holder, senior procurement manager, and Jack Grossman, VP of technology."

Everyone on the presentation team had done their homework, researching LinkedIn profiles and other background information on company websites and social media, so they recognized the players at the table. Susan seemed warm and welcoming, and Bill, though poised and reserved, smiled broadly. Stephanie was polite but stiff, and Jack was clearly doing the bare minimum. In fact, his behavior bordered on smug. Paul smiled at the MFS IT staff seated behind the table. His team had worked with them recently on a proof of concept, and they had been professional and friendly. A few offered half smiles, but Susan's three Worldwide IT staff members waved and nodded warmly. Paul's team had worked closely with them over the past several years, and he nodded back at them with a grin. He scanned the room as he sat down and couldn't help thinking, *I hope none of these people play poker. I know the exact cards everyone's holding!* His emotions, confident but nervous, were an odd mix. The team was as prepared as they could be, but he still wished he could have been a fly on the wall during the earlier JCN presentation.

MEGA FINANCIAL SYSTEMS

**Integrate the Worldwide
Acquisition Ahead of Schedule
and the AIC Acquisition Quickly
at the Lowest Cost**

· **Ag*i*le**

Steeling his nerves, Paul took the reins. "Thank you all very much for your time today. We really appreciate the opportunity to present to you, and we're confident that we can show you an approach that will foster a true win/win dynamic as we work together. For the next ninety minutes we'd like to set aside the typical rules and format for this kind of presentation—you know, the kind where we talk and you listen." He paused to let the curiosity build a bit. "Instead, we'd like to have a dialogue with you."

Susan and her team smiled in anticipation of what lay ahead. They had already seen this type of presentation from Agile and had come to enjoy it. Bill leaned forward, his interest clearly piqued. But Jack and Stephanie sat stoically, letting Paul know in no uncertain terms that however he wanted to characterize the next hour and a half, it would be an uphill climb.

MFS's Objectives

- Complete Worldwide integration by Board's deadline or sooner
- Provide MFS Sales access to all Worldwide data and applications
- Minimize disruption to current MFS IT operations
- Minimize downtime after implementation
- Complete within budget
- Complete AIC integration as quickly as possible and minimize costs
- Create technology solutions and capabilities to enable future acquisitions

. . . . Ag*i*le

As soon as Paul clicked the second slide into view, Susan leaned in, sensing an opportunity to win a political point or two. "You're absolutely right to make the deadline the first item on this slide. It is critically important to MFS that we get this done on time." She and Bill also confirmed that MFS would require access to *all* Worldwide data and applications at the go-live date—not just a prioritized part of the data.

Paul was off to a good start, getting immediate confirmation of two important issues and setting a positive tone out of the gate. But as he touched on the importance of minimizing disruption to current MFS IT operations, Jack shifted and stiffened in his seat. "So by 'minimizing disruption,'" he started in, heavily air-quoting the words, "are you suggesting that my people are not up to the task of managing the integration from our end?"

Uhf, I've stepped in it now, and only five minutes in, Paul thought. *Of course* that's not what he meant, but neither he nor anyone on his team had anticipated this kind of response. The MFS VP was clearly planting his flag on the far side of the field. Susan and Bill watched Paul intently. He needed to manage this by himself, and Paul knew this was an opportunity to pick up some style points.

"Not at all, Jack," Paul responded, his tone direct but polite. "In fact, we know that your staff will need to carry out the critical jobs they are doing today throughout the integration period. In our experience at Agile, a successful integration requires a dedicated team working in concert with everyday activities to minimize disruption to the business. When the integration is complete, we assume that MFS wants the uptime for revenue-generating applications to be as high as possible."

Hearing this, Jack relaxed a bit and sat back in his chair.

He nodded, face neutral, knowing he had lost a tactical point but no less set in his strategy. Susan and Bill telegraphed their approval by looking away from Jack to the screen, as if to say, *good, let's move on.*

Bill was eager to address the next bullet, and he jumped in, "Paul, I know the next item is pretty pro forma, but getting this done under budget is even more important than before. With the recent AIC announcement, our CEO is keen to minimize the costs of integrating both AIC and Worldwide, as you might expect. With that in mind, how do you plan to both meet the deadline and keep integration costs within budget?"

This was a logical question that had to be asked, and having Bill speak it out loud played right into Paul's hands.

"Great question, Bill," Paul continued. "We've definitely anticipated the pressure that the new acquisition will put on costs. To handle this, we're going to propose an option to minimize both the expense and time frame of the integration."

"How are you going to pull that off?" Jack interrupted. "Are you aware that AIC outsources their IT and all of their infrastructure to JCN?"

Paul had hoped to have this part of the discussion when

he presented the options, but with Jack clearly playing "opposing counsel" and pushing back at every chance, he needed to be quick on his feet. Thankfully, he was prepared; he just hoped that Bill would like the plan he and Susan had put together.

Turning to Jack, Paul said, "Yes, our team is aware of AIC's relationship with JCN, and to control costs we propose using the existing IT staff and expertise at Worldwide to manage the AIC integration, with minimal additional integration support from Agile."

"Really?" Jack huffed. "Where did *this* idea come from, and why is this the first I've heard of it?" He shot a withering look in Susan's direction. This reaction was expected, and thanks to their work with Susan, Paul and his team were prepared. At least openly-hostile Jack was a clearer adversary than pretending-to-be-civil Jack. Still, Paul wondered what other political undercurrents were at play in the room.

"Susan, is this really a viable alternative?" Bill asked.

"Yes," she responded quickly. "Our team has investigated this option and we're confident we can pull it off using Agile's technology with no additional hardware costs and minimal additional integration support from Agile. After all," she continued, turning to Jack, "our team has been doing it successfully this way for years."

"Well if that's true," Bill said, looking pleased, "it's the best news I've heard all day!"

Paul had beat back another advance from Jack, but this would clearly not be the last skirmish in today's turf war. He was beginning to sense the rhythm of Jack's strategy, and he girded himself for more. "Finally," he continued, "Agile has the right technology solutions and capabilities to support future acquisitions."

"Of *course* Agile is the *right solution*," Jack interjected, right on cue. "Just like JCN was the *right solution* just a couple hours ago. So how can both Agile *and* JCN be the *right solution?*"

Paul was prepared for some studied objections from Jack, but each mocking repetition of *right solution* pushed his once ironic tone into outright sarcasm. Jack was a known JCN supporter, and he was clearly trying to keep the Agile team squarely in the "Sales 101" box—just another company with a good slide deck, predictable talking points, and well-dressed presenters. The fact is, if Paul's team had not done their homework and prepared the way they did, Jack would be right. After all, the first part of today's slide deck was, at least in structure, fairly conventional—and they *were* well dressed. But without knowing it, Jack had nicely teed up the part of today's discussion that would, with a little luck, begin to show the power of Agile's unique approach to both presenting and proposing.

"That's a great question, Jack," Paul responded, using his best boardroom *aikido*. "But we all have to say that, right? I mean, you wouldn't respect us if we didn't." This got a welcome laugh from *almost* everyone in the room. Paul hadn't answered the question, but he clearly set the expectation that his team had brought something different. Now they just had to execute!

"In fact, JCN *would* be the best solution in *some* cases. What we want to demonstrate to you today is that Agile is the *better* solution in *almost all* cases."

Already, Paul had begun to cut a hole in the box that Jack was trying so hard to keep him in. No one in this room had ever heard a presenter suggest that their competition would be the right solution for *anything*. It just wasn't done, and this candid admission shifted the energy, setting the stage for the rest of the presentation.

"How could you possibly know that?" Jack asked, the scold in his voice showing that he was far from done. But Paul had put an important stake in the ground, and as he turned and nodded to Doug Hand, he noted a smile on Susan's face. More important, Bill Sellers, the man they needed most to impress today, was leaning in. The steering committee's buy-in was critical, and more than any other player, Bill held the key to their success.

Taking Paul's cue, Doug rose with a short stack of reports and quickly distributed them to the stakeholders in the room. "This report looks at financial companies in the size range that MFS is most likely to acquire," he explained, "and it shows that these companies overwhelmingly use non-JCN IT infrastructures. In fact, only 12 percent of companies in this profile use JCN."

"Susan, are you aware of this data?" Bill asked, eyebrows arching.

"Yes, Bill. This is one of the major reasons Worldwide has chosen to standardize on Agile's technology. In fact, Agile has made it possible for us to quickly integrate new acquisitions, whether they were using JCN technology or not."

Bill considered her response for a moment. Susan Renly's talents and passion as CIO had been instrumental in making Worldwide an acquisition target for MFS, and both her experience and opinions were not to be ignored. "I've got to be honest with you," he admitted, "The steering committee has not discussed these implications for future acquisitions. Doug, this is a really valuable insight. Thank you. We need to bring this into the conversation."

Bill's response to Doug made Jack visibly uncomfortable. Paul caught him shifting in his chair and thought, *so far so good, but this one's just regrouping!*

Jack's rise to VP status had not been by accident, building his career on a foundation of real technical knowledge, profit-building outcomes, and better-than-average people skills (hardly on display today). But like so many of his peers, he worked hard to reconcile his skillful but largely "left brain" path to power with the deeply strategic and political demands of his position. And when Susan made the point about future acquisitions, he was caught off guard. Like a right fielder who had shuffled too close to first, expecting a bunt, he was now sprinting for the wall. Agile had put a fastball across the plate, belt-high, and Susan had cracked a hit deep into right.

When the third slide clicked into view, Jack almost jumped out of his seat. This was an "easy out."

"What makes Agile think they can tell an organization the size of MFS what should be important to them in a deal?", Jack demanded. "And isn't it a bit presumptuous to assume we will do a deal with you?" He had only read the title, of course, but his outburst stirred Stephanie Holder, the normally taciturn senior procurement manager at MFS, who nodded aggressively in agreement.

"That's not the intent at all," Tim Rosser said, speaking up for the first time.

With two opposing voices now in the conversation, Tim, Agile's VP of sales, felt it was the right time to jump in. "One of the reasons I'm here, in fact, is to more fully understand what is important to MFS so that we can ensure that Agile is prepared to deliver it. The point of this slide is to initiate a conversation so that rather than just giving you our opinion of what's right for MFS, we can come to those conclusions together."

"Calm down, Jack, and let's have a look at this slide," Bill interjected, smiling. "We might actually learn something." This got a few muted chuckles, eased the tension a bit, and brought everyone's focus back to the presentation. "After all," he continued, "Paul's team has already shown us that they're thinking ahead. Until today we hadn't considered future acquisitions, so I'm not convinced that we've fully thought through everything on this list."

Paul pushed forward, reviewing each MFS outcome and Agile deal lever with the now-attentive table. Susan and Bill agreed that, as far as they were concerned, these were the right items. Pressed by Bill, even Jack agreed that it was a valid list. This was a key stepping stone. Paul asked about the priorities his team had assigned to the outcomes in the list, which prompted a fair amount of discussion among the MFS steering committee principals.

Finally, Bill spoke up, "Paul, I appreciate the clear way you've linked your services to the outcomes we want to achieve. That's been very helpful. There's only one significant change that I see. We'd like the AIC acquisition to be moved up to number two on the list. Now that the announcement is public, I can share with everyone that our CEO is really pushing to close the deal with AIC as quickly as possible. In fact, their board is meeting this weekend to approve the deal."

Paul nodded in agreement as he glanced at the faces of his team members. He was thankful for the detailed preparation they had done for this meeting. This discussion was really paying off.

What Is Important to Agile in this Deal

1. Worldwide storage and software (Dataccess) discount
2. Adequate level of Implementation Services to meet deadline
3. Training for minimum 10 MFS IT staff
4. Deal close in two weeks to meet Board deadline
5. Appropriate level of support after implementation
6. Payment up front
7. Contract term (longer is better)
8. Quarterly Customer Value Reviews with SVP and CIO
9. Storage, software, and support for AIC acquisition
10. Public awareness (references, co-publish papers, conferences)

. . . . **Ag*i*le**

When Paul clicked the fourth slide into view, Stephanie Holder finally spoke. "Why should I care what's important to Agile in this deal?" she said stiffly. "And why should the steering committee care, for that matter? As far as I'm concerned, we're here to accomplish what's in the best interests of MFS."

Clearly not gunning for style points, Stephanie had jumped into the pit. "How is this not a waste of time?" she pressed. "The fourth bullet is self-evident. Closing the deal in two weeks means before the end of the quarter for Agile, so *of course* you want the deal closed by then. Why don't we just jump to the pricing?"

Bill moved to talk, but Tim politely broke in, "I'm sorry to interrupt, but I'd like to speak to this." Addressing Stephanie directly, he said, "I can see where you might make that connection, but in fact, the close date is based on beating the deadline set by the MFS board. And as we'll demonstrate, if the deal closes on time, we can *substantially beat that deadline*. The truth is, Agile would prefer to close the deal *next* quarter. Our business has grown over 18 percent this quarter, we are well ahead of Wall Street expectations, and pushing the close for this deal back would give us a great head start on next quarter."

Jack and Stephanie sat back, incredulous. Neither would come right out and call Tim a liar, but they found it hard to believe that Agile would offer this level of accommodation. Before they could respond, Bill broke in. "I'm interested in what Agile has to say on this slide," he said, his own voice tinged with doubt. "I'm curious because I've never seen a supplier take time to explain what was important to them in a deal. And I'd like to remind my fellow committee members of how much time we've spent in the past arguing over this very topic. At best, we've only ever come up with educated guesses."

Paul was grateful that Bill was steering a middle path in this meeting, allowing his team to stay on topic, follow their agenda, and keep a rich dialogue going, even if it occasionally veered into brinkmanship. Clearly Bill held the power in the room, and the way he wielded it showed why. Paul just needed to be sure he played to that power while still being respectful of the "opposing counsel."

Bill led the discussion now as they moved through the

slide, occasionally asking Susan for clarification on technical questions. Finally, turning to Paul, he said, "Thank you for this. Like I said, we've never seen a supplier offer this kind of information, and you may have just raised the bar for what I expect from a partner that wants to work long-term with MFS."

Paul smiled broadly and nodded, echoing nods from Tim and Susan, while the paperwork in front of Stephanie and Jack seemed to have drawn their attention from the conversation.

Past Value Delivered by Agile

- Completed Global Financial Solutions integration for Worldwide in five weeks—three weeks ahead of schedule
- Completed International Assets Corp. integration for Worldwide in three weeks—six weeks ahead of schedule
- Completed integration of Smith Financial Planning and Jones Investments merger within one month—two months ahead of schedule
- Completed two simultaneous acquisitions for Signet Investments three months ahead of schedule, eliminating need for new hardware

· **Ag*i*le**

Unlike the previous two slides, the fifth failed to induce any sudden chair calisthenics from Jack or Stephanie. Bill asked questions around the circumstances of each of Agile's past integration efforts and what similarities they shared with the Worldwide and AIC integrations. Susan added insight into the first and second bullets as she and her team were involved in these projects. When

Jack asked how these were relevant, technically, to the current Worldwide integration, Doug responded that there were many technical similarities, and he ticked them off one-by-one. Doug also warned about some of the pitfalls the team would need to look out for during the Worldwide integration.

Bill listened intently, and as Doug wrapped his explanation, Paul noticed Jack's body language shift and relax a bit, with the faintest suggestion of a nod. Was it a nod of approval or resignation? Not clear, but the momentum seemed to have shifted to Paul's favor—and just in time for the most important part of the presentation.

Options for Moving Forward

	Complete Worldwide Integration Ahead of Schedule	Complete Worldwide and AIC Ahead of Schedule (at lowest cost)	Complete Worldwide and AIC Ahead of Schedule (plus future acquisitions)
Solution	Agile Dataccess cost: $13.68M	Agile Dataccess cost: $15.75M	Agile Dataccess cost: $17.77M
Schedule	5 weeks from contract signing	Worldwide: 5 weeks; AIC: 8 weeks from contract signing	Worldwide: 5 weeks; AIC: 8 weeks (future acquisition TBD)
Discount	31.6%	34.7%	38.3%
Implementation Services	15 Agile Service Engineers Cost: $920K	17 Agile Service Engineers Cost: $1.06M	17 Agile Service Engineers, 3 Agile Engineers on staff (3 years) Cost: $1.65M (yr 1), $590K (yrs 2-3)
Worldwide IT Staff Training	10 MFS IT staff onsite Cost: $80K	10 MFS IT staff onsite Cost: $80K	14 MFS IT staff onsite Cost: $112K
Platinum Support	Dedicated staff and call-in number 24/7 Cost: $240K annually	Dedicated staff and call-in number 24/7 Cost: $240K annually	Dedicated staff and call-in number 24/7 Cost: $240K annually
Contract Term	1 year	2 years	3 years
Software Maintenance	1 year	2 years	3 years
Payment Terms	100% up front	75% up front / 25% at completion of AIC integration	3 equal payments at the beginning of each year
Other Items	2 References, jointly present 1 Conference Paper	4 References, 2 Conference Papers, 1 Case Study	6 References, 3 Conference Papers, 2 Case Studies

Ag*i*le

Paul clicked to the next slide to set up the discussion. Addressing the room, he began, "As we review the options for moving forward, I want to stress that these are just the options that Agile has developed to date. By no means are they the only ones available to MFS and Agile." He asked everyone to hold their questions until he had presented an overview of each option, and then they could get into as much detail as they wanted.

As Paul began reviewing the details of the first option, Bill interrupted, apologetic but animated, and asked if Paul was sure that Agile could complete the Worldwide integration in five weeks. Paul said that, based on all the information shared to date, they were one hundred percent confident in this number.

Bill turned to Susan, who echoed Paul's assessment. "Then I want to amend something I said earlier," Bill responded, without irony. "*This* is the best news I've heard all day!"

Paul gauged the situation carefully, and after walking through the three options, he asked the MFS steering committee which one they thought best met their current needs. Susan looked on expectantly. The shift in momentum seemed almost too good to be true, but he was certain that Jack and Stephanie, who were consumed in an intense, hushed conversation, were just rebuilding steam.

"I'm obviously focused on the second option," Bill responded, "but I'm also interested in the third. The larger discount is fine, but I'm very intrigued by the prospect of putting in place a plan to address not just the current integrations, but future acquisitions as well."

Abruptly, Bill turned to his huddled table mates. "Stephanie, Jack, would you like to share your conversation with the group." His voice was calm and tinged with humor, but before either could answer, Bill followed up with a more constructive request. "Which of these options do you like best? Which do you think best meets the needs of MFS?"

Jack had spent most of the time on this slide in a scrum with Stephanie, the two of them now combining their tactics against Agile's unconventional strategy. In the end, JCN's approach, and by extension Jack's, to getting this business was the classic "hammer looking for a nail." It was all about price. So far, Paul had skillfully steered the conversation away from money and toward *value* through meeting the board's deadline. This had coaxed a conversation from the Senior VP at MFS that brought a novel and constructive dynamic to the presentation.

Finally, Jack swung his hammer. "Without vetting the viability of Agile's scheme of using the Worldwide team for the AIC integration," he argued, "there's no way I can support options two or three. As for number one, dealing with only the Worldwide integration, every single cost on this option is unnecessary. JCN has just offered the software and services to handle both the Worldwide *and* AIC integrations *for free!*"

Jack had hit the pricing "nail" as squarely as he could, hoping to drive it home, and though Paul suspected it was coming, the resonance and power of the word "free" put him back on his heels. After all, no matter how one reasons that *free is never really free*, the word still packs a punch, especially when it's offered as the cost, or lack of, for two full IT integrations!

But Bill quickly spoke up, "Jack, I need to remind you that as a committee we agreed not to discuss either supplier's presentation in the presence of the other. In fact, it was Stephanie who insisted on it. And calling Agile's approach to the AIC integration a 'scheme' is inappropriate and, frankly, inaccurate in my opinion. I find their proposal to show ingenuity and a welcome spirit of collaboration. It's exactly the thinking I'm looking for from both the supplier *and the steering committee.*"

He spoke the last four words slowly, looking first at Jack, then at Stephanie, to whom he directed a final question. "Stephanie do you have any objections or comments about these options?"

The procurement manager said no but allowed that she was "disturbed" by what she called the insultingly low discounts Agile was currently offering MFS, as well as their "outrageous" demand for upfront payment. Bill thanked her and said that she could take up both concerns with Agile when *and if* they were selected.

Again, Bill's measured words and delivery showed his mastery of the room and leadership skill, at once mollifying Stephanie by assuring her that a choice had yet to be made and that her concerns would be considered, while letting Paul know that in spite of the positive tone of the presentation thus far, Agile was not a shoo-in.

Through all of this, Susan remained silent and watchful. Paul knew she had his back, but she also had her own agenda, and he wondered how all of this would play out for her and others politically.

Summary

Our goal was to provide MFS solutions to...

* Complete Worldwide integration ahead of deadline
* Provide MFS Sales access to all Worldwide data and applications
* Minimize disruption to current MFS IT staff
* Maximize uptime after implementation
* Complete all work under MFS budget
* Complete AIC integration ahead of schedule at lowest cost
* Provide technology solutions to enable future acquisitions

. . . . **Agile**

Finally, it was time to wrap the presentation. Jack and

Stephanie had spelled out "P-R-I-C-E" in bright, exploding letters in the night sky, and Bill had made a strong case for the value that Agile was proposing to bring, not least in their collaborative approach to the sale and integration itself. Both perspectives were valid and worthy of serious further consideration. One way or another, the solutions proposed by Agile and JCN would cost MFS, but Paul felt good that he and his team, with a little help from Bill, had accomplished what they set out to do today.

Paul closed with a summary detailing the goals for today's meeting, emphasizing that Agile had provided the steering committee clear and timely solutions for the integrations of Worldwide and AIC. Susan and Bill were attentive and engaged, and they confirmed that Agile had indeed accomplished these goals. Jack and Stephanie sat silent, having said their piece.

"Paul, on behalf of the steering committee I want to thank you and your team for an excellent and unusual presentation today," Bill concluded, glancing at the clock, "and also let you know that we will have a decision before the end of the day. We'll be in touch."

"Thank you, Bill, it's been our pleasure," Paul responded, hiding his surprise. He had been under the impression that a decision would take up to a week, and now this would change their agenda for the remainder of the day. The meeting broke up quickly. Jack offered Paul a half smile and a quick handshake before hustling out the door with Stephanie. Bill and Susan offered warm smiles and congratulations on a "terrific presentation and discussion."

Bill turned to Tim Rosser and said, "I've seen hundreds of supplier proposal presentations, and this was by far the best. Your team showed an understanding of the real issues facing my company, and I really appreciate your collaborative approach to choosing a solution. It was such a relief from the 'all-about-us, take-it-or-leave-it' norm." Tim smiled and thanked Bill, assuring him that Paul and the team deserved most of the credit.

For his part, Paul was less sanguine. He had seen too many companies, bedazzled by the "price" fireworks, go with the lowest bidder, agreeing with the Jacks and Stephanies who insisted that any approach that didn't address cost head-on—as a singular, all-important driver—was inherently dishonest, underhanded, or simply naïve. He was hopeful but wouldn't allow himself to assume they had won the day. The kind of prospective partner who could understand and embrace a more strategic concept of value would be the one most likely to choose Agile, based on today's style of presentation. Paul could only hope that MFS was that partner, and that Susan had guided him and his team well.

With a smile and a final word of thanks, Susan told Paul to expect a call by the end of the day. She or Bill would let him know the outcome of today's meeting. Paul and the team gathered in the lobby as Tim shook hands and congratulated everyone on a great presentation.

Making their way to the door, Tim said to Paul, "You're buying lunch, but you can pick the place."

"It's good to have options," Paul deadpanned, and they both chuckled.

"You really rocked it today," Tim added. "It was rough going in places and I tried to help where I could, but you held your ground. Jack and Stephanie had a lot at stake, and they were guarding the fort at all costs, even if it made them look bad."

Tim stopped walking and turned to Paul, "You know that if we win, you're going to be negotiating with Stephanie, right?"

Paul's laugh was resigned but deep and real, and it was the only answer Tim needed. They shook hands, and as Tim got in his car, he told Paul that he wanted to attend the negotiation strategy meeting, which needed to happen Monday morning, and to be sure to keep him posted on scheduling.

Tim's cheeky, presumed close lightened Paul's mood a bit.

* * *

The call came in at 4:00 on the button.

"Paul, that was an impressive performance today," Bill began. "But..."

"Uh-oh," Paul cringed.

"...nothing. It was practically perfect," Bill laughed, "and we look forward to working with you and the Agile team on the integrations!"

"Thank you, Bill," Paul exclaimed, genuinely surprised and palpably relieved. "We're honored to be working with you and I really appreciate your thoughtful input today. If you don't mind my asking, which option did MFS find most...?"

"Number three," Bill said before Paul could finish. He was ready to move forward and no longer concerned about hiding his enthusiasm. "We would like to make one small change and that is to reduce the implementation services, for now anyway, to the level you had in the second option. I'd like you to incorporate it into the final written proposal as I only want to commit funds to the Worldwide and AIC integrations at this point. Also, you'll be negotiating with Stephanie, and you two can hammer out rates and other details for any future acquisitions. I hope this is agreeable to Agile. We need to make it happen no later than Tuesday, and I want a signed contract and work started as soon as possible after that."

"That works for us," Paul responded without hesitation. "You'll have the formal written proposal no later than Monday morning." He was elated as much by the news as by the pleasure and privilege of congratulating his team. They would have a hard weekend of work ahead to finish the written proposal in time, but that would not get in the way of tonight's celebration. And he'd be sure to raise a sincere toast to Jack and Stephanie. Jack fought hard and lost, but now Stephanie would be his counterpart in what promised to be a challenging negotiation.

Might as well savor the moment and assume the best for next week!

Summary

Your proposal is one of the most powerful ways you can differentiate yourself and your company from the competition. It also facilitates what I term one of the *critical conversations* in the Value Lifecycle™, namely, the ongoing business relationship. The main purpose of the compelling proposal is to bridge from selling (creating value) to negotiating (capturing value). In short, your proposal has the potential to make you and your company look very different—in a good way. Done well, it ensures you are making the *right* sale and setting up the *right* negotiation.

The fourth book in the *Must-Win Deals* series, *The Painless Negotiation*, will pick up where we left off today. How will Paul and Agile prepare for what is shaping up to be a very tough negotiation with Stephanie? What negotiation tactics and tricks does Stephanie have up her sleeve? How will Paul and the team respond? And let's not forget about JCN. Do you think they will take this loss lying down? How can Paul capture the value he and the team have created in a great deal that is good for both Agile and MFS? Stay tuned to see if Agile's team can deliver on their promise!

The final book in the series, *Can't-Lose Accounts*, will explore the management of the Value Lifecycle™ from the perspective of delivering the promised value and getting credit for delivering that value. How do you go about turning your company into a value managing machine? How can management "change the conversation" from an inward-looking view to one of value—for both your company and your customers? I hope you'll stay with me on this journey—we're more than half-way there!

> My goal in writing this book is to help you to see that how you propose your solution is just as important as the solution itself. This is consistent with my observation, time and again, that how you sell and negotiate deals is more important than what you sell—a crucial point that creates real job security for salespeople. Remember, your goal is to build trust and credibility through your proposal, while making it easy for the customer to choose you and your company.

While the compelling proposal template presented in this book has proven very successful, just remember that your proposal presentation is also an opportunity to differentiate yourself and your company by making the proposal process a "story"—one that can even be a surprising discovery for the customer. Use and change the template as you see fit for your business, bearing in mind that more is not necessarily better—especially when it is about your company. *The proposal is not about you*, and however you go about it, if you are not advancing the objectives detailed in this book, then you must question what you are changing or adding to it. In other words, tell the *customer's story* in a concise, engaging, and easily digestible way that makes it easier for them to *buy*!

As a point of balance, it's worth noting that your customer is likely to have fairly low expectations for your proposal. While this statement may seem to qualify both the premise and value of this book, rest assured it does not—for two important reasons. First, even an imperfect effort on your part to build and present a compelling proposal will positively differentiate you from your competitor(s). Second, you can expect to get credit for attempting to make this stage of the selling process more engaging and even helpful to your customer. With practice and time will come proficiency at producing effective proposals, then it should begin to feel like second nature—and you will wonder why you ever did it differently.

If you'd like a free PowerPoint template for the proposal presentation, it can be downloaded free from my website, valuelifecycle.com. How's that for a value?

WANT MORE?

As a final bonus for you, I have developed a companion online workshop to this book, also titled *The Compelling Proposal*. It is available online at mustwindeals.valuelifecycle.com. If you're interested in working on your proposal by applying the concepts in these pages—something I highly recommend—please check it out. There are two tiers that include a standalone online workshop and a second version that also includes live one-on-one coaching from me on your live proposal. I am pleased to offer you a significant discount on either tier as a *thank you* for buying this book. Just enter the promotion code "**Book319**" to get your discount—and thanks for being a customer!

Good Selling!

About the Author

 **STEVE THOMPSON** is managing partner at Value Lifecycle™, which helps companies position, negotiate, and close critical business deals. In the past twenty years, he has worked on more than $15 billion in B2B deals in over 120 different industries. He previously worked in senior operations, sales, and executive management at Westinghouse, Black & Decker, and DuPont. Steve also served as a nuclear submarine officer in the US Navy.

Appendix

MFS
MEGA FINANCIAL SYSTEMS

Integrate the Worldwide
Acquisition Ahead of Schedule
and the AIC Acquisition Quickly
at the Lowest Cost

Ag*i*le
INFORMATION SOLUTIONS

MFS's Objectives

- Complete Worldwide integration by Board's deadline or sooner
- Provide MFS Sales access to all Worldwide data and applications
- Minimize disruption to current MFS IT operations
- Minimize downtime after implementation
- Complete within budget
- Complete AIC integration as quickly as possible and minimize costs
- Create technology solutions and capabilities to enable future acquisitions

Ag*i*le

Important to MFS in Our Deal

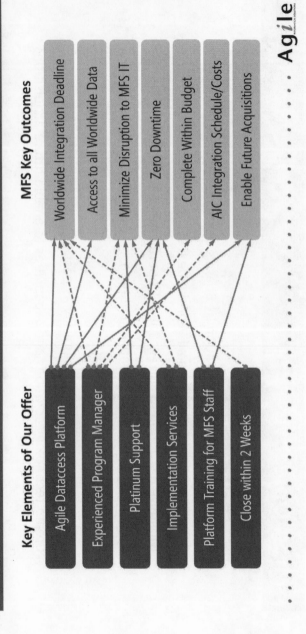

Key Elements of Our Offer

- Agile Dataccess Platform
- Experienced Program Manager
- Platinum Support
- Implementation Services
- Platform Training for MFS Staff
- Close within 2 Weeks

MFS Key Outcomes

- Worldwide Integration Deadline
- Access to all Worldwide Data
- Minimize Disruption to MFS IT
- Zero Downtime
- Complete Within Budget
- AIC Integration Schedule/Costs
- Enable Future Acquisitions

Agile

What Is Important to Agile in this Deal

1. Worldwide storage and software (Dataccess) discount
2. Adequate level of Implementation Services to meet deadline
3. Training for minimum 10 MFS IT staff
4. Deal close in two weeks to meet Board deadline
5. Appropriate level of support after implementation
6. Payment up front
7. Contract term (longer is better)
8. Quarterly Customer Value Reviews with SVP and CIO
9. Storage, software, and support for AIC acquisition
10. Public awareness (references, co-publish papers, conferences)

Agile

Past Value Delivered by Agile

- Completed Global Financial Solutions integration for Worldwide in five weeks—three weeks ahead of schedule

- Completed International Assets Corp. integration for Worldwide in three weeks—six weeks ahead of schedule

- Completed integration of Smith Financial Planning and Jones Investments merger within one month—two months ahead of schedule

- Completed two simultaneous acquisitions for Signet Investments three months ahead of schedule, eliminating need for new hardware

Options for Moving Forward

	Complete Worldwide Integration Ahead of Schedule	Complete Worldwide and AIC Ahead of Schedule (at lowest cost)	Complete Worldwide and AIC Ahead of Schedule (plus future acquisitions)
Solution	Agile Dataccess cost: $13.68M	Agile Dataccess cost: $15.75M	Agile Dataccess cost: $17.77M
Schedule	5 weeks from contract signing	Worldwide: 5 weeks; AIC: 8 weeks from contract signing	Worldwide: 5 weeks, AIC: 8 weeks (future acquisition TBD)
Discount	31.6%	34.7%	38.3%
Implementation Services	15 Agile Service Engineers Cost: $920K	17 Agile Service Engineers Cost: $1.06M	17 Agile Service Engineers, 3 Agile Engineers on staff (3 years) Cost: $1.65M (yr 1), $590K (yrs 2-3)
Worldwide IT Staff Training	10 MFS IT staff onsite Cost: $80K	10 MFS IT staff onsite Cost: $80K	14 MFS IT staff onsite Cost: $112K
Platinum Support	Dedicated staff and call-in number 24/7 Cost: $240K annually	Dedicated staff and call-in number 24/7 Cost: $240K annually	Dedicated staff and call-in number 24/7 Cost: $240K annually
Contract Term	1 year	2 years	3 years
Software Maintenance	1 year	2 years	3 years
Payment Terms	100% up front	75% up front / 25% at completion of AIC integration	3 equal payments at the beginning of each year
Other Items	2 References, jointly present 1 Conference Paper	4 References, 2 Conference Papers, 1 Case Study	6 References, 3 Conference Papers, 2 Case Studies

Agile

Summary

Our goal was to provide MFS solutions to...

- Complete Worldwide integration ahead of deadline
- Provide MFS Sales access to all Worldwide data and applications
- Minimize disruption to current MFS IT staff
- Maximize uptime after implementation
- Complete all work under MFS budget
- Complete AIC integration ahead of schedule at lowest cost
- Provide technology solutions to enable future acquisitions

Ag*i*le